Paper Tiger

Paper Tiger

Original drawings by Jasun Horsley
Photoshop & design by Lucinda Horan

Paper Tiger
Copyright © Jasun Horsley 2010

Cover design by Lucinda Horan

Other works by Jasun Horsley:

Seen & Not Seen: Confessions of a Movie Autist
Dark Oasis: A Self-Made Messiah Unveiled
Prisoner of Infinity: UFOs, Social Engineering, and Psychic Fragmentation (2018)
The Vice of Kings: Occultism, Social Control, Abuse Culture (2018)

Foreword to 2013 Edition

Written in March of 2010, *Paper Tiger* is about my relationship to my brother, the late artist Sebastian Horsley (although his name is never mentioned in the text), and includes references to his memoir, *Dandy in the Underworld*. At the time I wrote it, we weren't speaking to each other due to disagreements over our mother's will. (She had recently been diagnosed with cancer.) I was angry with him, and writing the book was a way for me to disentangle from him by identifying the ways we had been "enmeshed" since childhood. It was a way to have a dialogue with my brother without his having to consent to it, or be actually present.

After *Paper Tiger* was printed (fifty copies), I sent a copy to my brother. He died of a heroin overdose, in June 2010, several days before it arrived. The reconciliation which I had hoped to bring about through writing the book did not happen anywhere but within my own psyche. But then, that is what the book was always about. I like to think that, in and through his death, we *were* reconciled. Certainly, as strange as this may sound, I feel closer to my brother since he died than I did while he was alive.

In a curious development, roughly two years after I wrote *Paper Tiger*, a West End show, *A Song Cycle for Soho*, opened, featuring an operatic number called "The Ballad of the Horsley Brothers." I discovered the song by chance, several months after the show had closed. I emailed the song's writer, Dougal Irvine, and he told me about the genesis of the work. He had known nothing about Sebastian or myself, he said, and had been given the following scenario by the show's writer: "Jason Horsley walks into a bar in Soho and spots a ghostly figure." Soho is the area in London my brother enjoyed his local celebrity, an area I rarely visit. I also never go to bars. Yet the song captured the spirit, if not letter, of our relationship.

It has been two and a half years since my brother died. He knew me better than any other man alive, and I miss him. I considered revising the book for this new edition, however slightly, but then I realized it would be to do it a disservice. What you're about to read is an unconscious goodbye, and thank you, to my brother as he prepared to leave this world. It would never have been as honest, or as direct, if I had known what I was doing at the time.

And although I am fairly sure he would have hated it while he was alive, I like to think that, in death, he is able to appreciate it.

Jasun Horsley, January 2013

CONTENTS

"When the stars threw down their spears,
And watered heaven with their tears,
Did he smile his work to see?
Did he who made the Lamb make thee?"
—William Blake, "The Tyger"

Jasun Horsley

My Brother, My Keeper

Dear Cain

I don't expect you to believe me, but none of this was my idea. I'm not angry at you for what you did. You were only following your nature, as I was mine. The story was predetermined from the start. You were written to play the slayer, as I was down to be the slain. As long as I was Abel, you had to be Cain.

Suicide by brother? I can't think of a better way to go. This is not just a goodbye note; it's also a thank you letter for all you have done. By being such a ferocious lion, you have led me to lie down with the lamb.

Thank you, brother, and fare thee well. Death is indeed the crown of all, and I couldn't have done it without you!

Abel

A Tale of Two Brothers

"And the LORD said unto Cain, Where is Abel thy brother? And he said, I know not: Am I my brother's keeper?"
—Genesis 4: 6-9

This is the tale of two brothers. I am one, the subject of this story is the other. Perhaps the strangest thing about this story is that, although it is my own, I am little more than a bystander in the narrative.

The forest is now empty, for the tree that fell landed right on top of the only one around to hear it. And so there *was* no sound, besides his cry.

What follows is the echo of that cry, as it is swallowed by the silence. It is a tale of brotherly love, and of brotherly violence.

There are two things I will say about my brother. The first is that he is without doubt the biggest asshole I have ever known, as well as my greatest, indeed only, enemy in this life.

The other is that, more than any person alive, he made me the man I am today.

He is both the hero and the villain of my story, while I am both his victim and his beneficiary.

Love comes in many guises. One thing that I can say about my love for my brother: it has never been lukewarm. After my father, he is the first man I ever loved, and the only man I ever hated.

He likes to refer to himself as "mediocrity on stilts"; the truth is more disturbing and complex than that. If much of what follows seems to be about the smallness of his spirit, that is only because I, more than any other, know the greatness that lies within his heart.

The Slayer & the Slain

"The greatest burden a child must bear is the unlived life of the parents."
—C.G. Jung

A word about myself. My mother loved me so much that she stunted my growth. Though I was never breast-fed, I was all but smothered by her embrace. Her love was not unconditional, you see. I was used as an even greater source of comfort to her than the bottle. I was not quite comfort enough to replace it, however; in fact, she was even drinking through my (unnaturally induced) birth. Considering the amount she drunk while I was in the womb, it is a wonder I didn't come out pickled.

I was for my mother what is known (these days) as "a husband surrogate child." I suppose that must have been quite nice for me at the time, getting to be the special one. But it can wreak havoc in a man's psyche later in life. I was forty before I realized that I had been attached to my mother by a psychic umbilical chord for my whole life.

Before I came along, my brother had been the only male child, so it is easy to imagine his consternation when I entered the picture and he found himself playing second fiddle to a golden-haired intruder. Our father was already indifferent to him, having favored our sister, the first-born. So my brother was caught in the middle, and doubly rejected, by both his father *and* his mother. I have no idea what it was like for him; I don't remember. But, judging by how my brother still bristles today, it seems safe to say that his bristling begun early in life. The situation must have been intolerable for him. Parents wound their children without even trying.

Is there more? My friends, there is so much more to this story that pretty soon you will be sorry you ever asked. I am not Dostoyevsky, however, so have no fear: this is not the start of a thousand-page novel of mother-bondage and fratricide. It is the start of a 14,000-word mythic narrative of mother-bondage and fratricide. I will try to keep to the main points, but please bear with me if I seem to ramble or digress. There are many layers to this narrative, for this is not only a personal story. It is also a blueprint. And if you read it closely enough, you may find this story is your own.

A Binary System

"I remember having a vision about my brother with whom my relationship had always been fraught—the usual sibling rivalries carried to some pretty nasty and petty extremes. He was, after all, a potential threat to my individuality. We like to speak casually about 'sibling rivalry' as though it were some kind of by-product of growing up, a bit of competitiveness and selfishness in children who have been spoilt, who haven't yet grown into a generous social nature. But it is too all-absorbing and relentless to be an aberration; it expresses the heart of the creature—the desire to stand out. Now, suddenly, I saw that the war was over. We flew together until we faced each other. I took off my head. He took off his. I placed mine on his shoulders and he placed his on mine. I have to say that I think he got the better deal."
—The Brother's Ibogaine experience, 2004

That my brother and I are polar opposites is a fact that has been evident to both of us for many years. The more he pulls in one direction, the more I am driven to the other extreme, and vice versa. I have lived most of my life as a virtual aesthete and a sometimes celibate. He has lived his life as a libertine dandy, a hedonist who has slept with a thousand whores. Pulling apart. I have always had a Christ complex; yet it was he who opted to be crucified. He has always wished to be the center of the Universe, yet it was I who wound up lobbying to be "the One." Pulling together. It is as if we are two parts of a single organism, a binary system in which the one pole is forever reacting to and compensating for the other. For years, I assumed this was something genetic, that we were, like twins, a single psyche split into two bodies. Now I know that it has less to do with genetic hardwiring than with those early, formative years outlined above, and whatever it was that occurred, during that mostly forgotten time.

Fittingly enough, the way in which this polarity has most obviously played out between us is in our "religious" beliefs. My brother is a nihilist who has turned himself into a sort of Luciferian embodiment of the denial of God: "Even if God existed, I wouldn't believe in Him." Although I have never been religious (our father's staunch atheism imprinted us both from an early age), I have spent most of my adult life on what might be called a quest for higher meaning, for the possibility of a reality beyond the sovereign self. Yet, since opposites meet in the extreme, my brother and I are actually quite alike in essence. Isn't questing after truth as sure a way to stay out of truth as a denial of truth? We were cast from the same mold and shaped in the same laboratory: that of our alcohol-infused, sexually promiscuous family circle. It is only *the ways in which we have reacted* to our environment that differ so radically.

The bitter pill of truth that both of us must now swallow is that, while steadfastly pulling in opposite directions, we have both wound up in the same place: living a false narrative, defined by the unconscious load we have been carrying, a load made up of the unlived lives of our parents.

Some Personal Background

"Think not that I came to send peace on the earth: I came not to send peace, but a sword. For I came to set a man at variance against his father, and the daughter against her mother ..."
—Matthew 10:34-35

I suffered from night terrors as a child, and repeated minor illnesses. This carried through into adulthood, with chronic body pains, sore throats, headaches, and constant fatigue. My childhood is mostly a barren wasteland, a shadowy void in which monsters seem to lurk. Our mother doesn't remember much of what happened, since most of her attention was taken up by alcohol and an obsessive fixation on two men. (Another binary system.) She refers to that time as "like a nightmare," without being able to account for this feeling with anything concrete. Oddly, my brother has a similar take: "It's as if something terrible happened," he says, while insisting that nothing ever did. As with murder, sometimes the only evidence is an absence.

As an adolescent and teenager I looked up to my brother and wanted to be just like him. As I grew up, I copied his interests, his taste in music, his style of dress. Although he subtly encouraged me in this by giving me his old clothes, records, and such, he also resented me for it. Eventually, I did manage to find my own persona. Or so I thought.

The persona that I created for myself in adolescence and adulthood was that of a writer and film buff. Although I dabbled in poetry as a teenager, my real focus was on writing film reviews and scripts (and even some amateur filmmaking). Later on, I developed an interest in Castaneda, Crowley and the occult (something I had also been drawn to as a teenager, but only briefly). It is curious to note that these two interests (film and the supernatural) seem to echo my brother's childhood obsession with Hammer horror films. When I was growing up, the walls of his bedroom were covered with gory images, making his room a source of terror and fascination for me. My brother's world, though menacing and foreboding, was a world I desperately wished to enter into.

In 2007, my brother published his "unauthorized autobiography." By that time, I had already published five books, three of which were about film, another of which was about the occult, and the most recent, *Matrix Warrior*, published in 2003, was a mixture of occult lore and movie analysis. The book was part of my testing the waters as to whether I was "the One," and the verdict, naturally enough, would depend on how well the book sold. The book tanked. I was not the One. My brother's book, on the other hand, was reviewed by all the major periodicals and quickly optioned for a movie adaptation.

With his first serious foray into writing, he had achieved the goal I had worked half my life to attain.

Mind Control and Body Pains

"All actual conspiracy theories aside, this is the postmodernist perspective of existence, positing as it does the invasion and fragmentation of the human psyche by external factors such as media imagery, simulacra, viruses of the mind, artificial reality. In the postmodern as well as the paranoid *weltanschauung*, we exist vicariously, living lives which are not our own but rather the products of an alien collective body or program, be it that of the media, the Church, the State, or 'ET mind controllers' (or artificial intelligence). . . . All this is really only the paranoid's metaphorical description of a phenomenon which pertains to consciousness: that what we take to be wholly familiar territory—namely our own minds and personalities— has long ago been occupied and we have succumbed passively to the enemy."
—Aeolus Kephas, *The Lucid View*

We all know that people who hear voices are crazy. Yet we talk to ourselves all day long, and not all of our internal dialogue is friendly. So where is the line to be drawn? If a voice were installed into our consciousness early enough, we might take it for our own voice, regardless of how antithetical it might be to us. This is the case for me. My brother's voice has been inside my head for as long as I can remember, but this is a fact I have only just come to recognize. All these years, I thought it was my own voice. I knew all about mind control and schizophrenia, but that was something that happened to other people (rather like child abuse). I imagine the reader feels much the same way.

Yet if I cast my mind back, I first became aware of this voice in my head in my mid-twenties, during the time I started writing seriously. I developed a habit of reading back what I had written *as if through my brother's eyes*, imagining what he would think of it. This was a rather odd habit because I was fully aware that what I was writing would be of no interest to him, that it was beneath his contempt. So why imagine him as my audience? You might say that I was using him as an imaginary foil, a way of testing out my arguments in my own mind, and no doubt this was part of it. But there was something else there, something that took me twenty years to get to. My brother was actually *inside my mind.* He had installed himself there, like an MKULTRA programmer, pulling my strings.

Fitting, then, that the truth finally came to the surface when I was reading about the links between mind control programs and serial killers. The book presented evidence that many of the more famous serial murderers had not acted alone, but were part of a larger network that included organized crime, drug rings, child pornography and snuff movies, and elements of the US military and intelligence groups. While reading the book, I found myself imagining my brother's scornful reaction throughout, like a ceaseless nagging in my skull. The fact was my brother *did* dismiss any such subjects whenever they came up between us, with scorn and derision and in such a way that I tended to quickly drop the subject in order to avoid conflict. I am sure you have experienced something similar with family members: it is normal enough to have opposing points of view, and to have arguments that are charged way beyond the importance of the subjects themselves. But this was something else. Here I was arguing with my brother and he wasn't even on the same continent as me! This went beyond the normal sort of family disagreement or sibling rivalry. It was closer to a kind of obsession. It was as though some part of me *needed* to have my point of view, my version of reality, acknowledged, and was butting heads with a counter narrative in order to achieve this. Strangest of all, I was butting heads with *myself.*

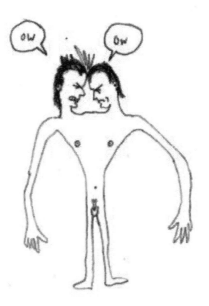

Jasun Horsley

Glamour Magik Vs. Grammar Magik

"I was the classic unreliable narrator whose passion to entertain overrode my duty to inform. My highly enameled prose was merely an extension of my rather gaudy clothes. I am not a writer. I am a performer. Writing is merely a way of bringing myself to the notice of the world. And it is the world I care about, not the writing."
—The Brother, in his Memoirs, 2007

It took me over two years to finally read my brother's book. I had dipped into the first chapter, and that had been enough. My brother's descriptions of our mother and other elements from my childhood seemed like deliberate distortions, designed for shock effect and easy laughs. Of course I looked for any references to myself. There were only two passages about me in the book, much to my relief. The longest was as follows:

"I was particularly horrible to my brother. It started early. When [my sister], coming back from the hospital, told me 'It's a boy,' my face fell to the floor. 'Stillborn' was kinda what I was hoping for. Jake was a potential threat to my individuality. From that moment on, my relationship with him was always fraught ~ any excuse I got to slap, stab, or shoot him, I took it. I remember pushing his pram down the sloping lawn and then letting it go to career into a ditch and turn over. 'Jake's dead I think,' I informed my mother. When he was older I used more subtle tactics. I remember kicking him in the stomach and watching him crumple like a deflating airbag. Once he was ostentatiously tapping his foot to Marc Bolan. I stood up and stamped on it. 'Find you own music,' I said. Later, he stole my clothes and possessions, trying to inhabit me. He failed. Nobody can be exactly like me. Even I have trouble doing it."

What my brother describes here is a fairly intense level of violence directed by one brother against another. Since there was almost five years difference between us, as the younger child, I would have been helpless to retaliate, at least for those first few years. Yet his description makes this intensely violent scenario seem of no real consequence, no more than rough play between siblings. It gives no hint of what it might have been like for me to be born under the shadow of such murderous rage. My brother's actions are hidden in plain sight, and this is the essence of his sorcery.

Here's another example. According to my brother, I was "a threat to [his] individuality." Actually, I was a threat to his *centrality* as the only son, and in reaction to that, he became a threat to *my own individuality*. In his version of the tale, since *I* am the threat, his attempt to murder me becomes "self-defense." The reader's sympathy remains with the protagonist, whose sovereignty remains unchallenged. It is telling also that my brother states that I was trying to "inhabit" him, when my experience is the reverse: it was he who inhabited me, possessed me, who occupied my thoughts and moods with his relentless violations.

The facts my brother presents are distorted by the force of his own perceptions. He projects his reality *onto* the facts, and thereby puts them in service to a false narrative. The reader sees but does not register what he sees, because his gaze is already being directed elsewhere. My brother's glamour magik was indeed extended onto the page. It had become *grammar* magik.

Since I am the most inconvenient detail in his life, he takes pains to reduce me to irrelevancy in his narrative. Erasure is the subtlest and most effective form of violence. I then become conspicuous for my absence. The only evidence of murder is that *there is no body to be found.*

How deeply installed is this false narrative in our family? Deep enough that it took almost forty years for my mother to realize that I had been bullied by my brother while we were growing up.

One thing that my brother does get right in his memoir is that our father was also most conspicuous by his absence, and largely indifferent to us as children. Both he and our mother were heavy drinkers and for much of the time oblivious to what we were doing. My brother has always been an intensely secretive individual, but even combining these factors, the reader may well ask: how did he ensure his treatment of me never come to our mother's attention? Somehow, he had to make me complicit, at least in keeping silent. To this day, I don't know how he managed it, but whatever went on during that time, my brother effectively pulled the wool over everyone's eyes, including my own. Even though his violent handling of me is now down in black and white in his memoir, I still find it hard to admit that any "abuse" occurred. It seems in bad taste to do so. After all, he has already "made light" of it.

The thing about cover stories is: they are never as interesting as what really happened. Who would want to read *Crime and Punishment* written by an unrepentant Raskolnikov? The truth is so much richer than that.

Jasun Horsley

Which Way is Up? The Rabbit Hole of Personal History

"When an inner situation is not made conscious, it appears outside as fate."
—C. G. Jung

The imposition of a false narrative begins the moment we are born, with the Cesarean birth, the induced contractions, or the moment we are slapped on the backside and forced to breathe. It continues when our mother tells us when to be hungry and when not to be; when not to cry and when to smile. We learn table manners and do what we are told. Infants are wild, instinctive creatures; they must be domesticated for their own good.

Our parents, already firmly inculcated with the correct modes of social behavior, indoctrinate us with the same "false narrative." Instinctive behavior is anti-social and must be suppressed. Social norms are imposed upon us from day one, rewarding us for meeting expectations (going along with the false narrative), and punishing us for failing to do so. Our fear of monsters is dismissed along with our imaginary friends; we are taught to be tough and resilient, and at the same time meek and obedient, in order to get along in the world. Adults *fear* the wildness of children. They project their fears *onto* the child and impose restrictions to protect it from their *own* (often imaginary) fears. This is called "good parenting."

The idea that, as instinctive creatures, infant children might know *exactly* what they need and when they need it (though not how to get it), this possibility is never allowed; and so the possibility of listening and responding to a child is reduced, in those early years, almost to zero. This then gives rise to impossibly demanding toddlers, and eventually, to impossibly demanding adults. Children who have not been heard, learn to make a lot of noise. Take my brother as an example. Or take me.

The physical, emotional, and psychological patterns we inherit as infants become our *narrative* as adults. Hardwired with *imprints instead of instincts,* our life trajectories have little or nothing to do with any conscious decisions on our part. We cling to these narratives as if our life depends on it, and to a certain extent it does. The way we view the world defines who we think we are: it is our constructed identity. Deconstructing these narratives then would be akin to identity suicide. Ideally, what we want is to construct and sustain a narrative in which we are Kings, sovereign royalty who get to decide the difference between right and wrong and in which everyone else slavishly agrees with us or suffers the consequences. This is a world that only A-list celebrities and the very, very rich ever get to experience: a world of Yes-people. Such a desire is a natural enough reaction to the powerlessness and anxiety we experience as children. The more intense the trauma of childhood (absent fathers, drunken mothers, bullying brothers, etc), the more desperately we cling to a compensatory narrative in which we have complete control and can feel totally safe.

How does this pertain to the present narrative?

My brother traffics in illusion. He does it quite well and has managed to charm his way onto book shelves and talk shows and may even wind up, one of these days, as a 50-foot Hollywood-incarnation at your local multiplex. Near the start of his book, citing how our Mother taught him the only thing worth knowing, he writes: "where there is contest between illusion and reality, reality should be requested to give in gracefully."

Like Lucifer, my brother creates false narratives in which he can be sovereign and supreme. He has done it since the day I was born, and he is still doing it today.

Jasun Horsley

Blueprint of a Wound

"Distant relatives are the best kind, and the further the better. You see, as a natural loner and auto-invention I grasped early the irrelevance of family life."
—The Brother, in 2007

My parents split up when I was seven and my brother was eleven or twelve. Before this, when I was only five, my mother took another lover (the man who eventually replaced my father). It's safe to say the marriage was nearing the rocks when I was born, and I think also safe to say that, as a result of this growing estrangement (as is often the case), my mother turned to her youngest son for comfort and well-being. My father might have experienced a degree of hostility towards the newborn as a result of this; but if so, it was my brother who received the brunt of it. The older the son, the more of a threat he is perceived to be, and the more suited a receptacle he is for the father's resentment. My brother is angry at our (deceased) father to this day, a feeling clearly expressed in his memoirs. It is perhaps the deepest wound he carries.

When my brother was young, our father scorned him for his stupidity, his perceived lack of intellect. My brother suffered from dyslexia, itself a likely symptom of stress; but there was little awareness of such a condition at the time. My brother eludes to this, while also glossing over it, when he writes: "I longed for dyslexia or some such alibi. Any attempts to dignify my idiocy where inevitably shot down by Father. 'Dyslexia is the term posh people use to describe their children's stupidity,' he would drawl." (This does not seem like a likely conversation between a father and a six-year-old.) My father's scornful dismissal of my brother for his stupidity would have cut extra deep, because our father continuously praised our sister for her intelligence. She was the only child our father showed interest in.

In his memoir, my brother describes how he learned to associate airy ruthlessness and distance with maleness, and passion with the female: "I searched myself for vestiges of masculinity as though for lice. I did not worry about my character but about my hair and clothes. . . . It took months but finally I had grown my hair as long as I could and tried with a yearning heart—and a few cunning simpers—to pass myself off as a girl." Our sister received from our father what my brother most desperately wanted. Like Dionysus, he came up with the most literal solution: to turn himself into a girl. As an unconscious attempt to appeal to our father, however, it was bound to backfire. He goes on to describe being caught by our father while dressed in our mother's clothing, miming to Marc Bolan, and how he crumpled in on himself and fell to the floor in embarrassment. His description is oddly echoed by his account of how I crumpled up "like a deflating airbag" when he kicked me.

As it happens, this incident is the earliest encounter with my brother that I remember in full. I was perhaps eight years old at the time, making my brother around twelve or thirteen, the age he lost his virginity (became a fully sexual being). I was coming up the stairs, berating him for a malicious prank he had played on me, when he kicked me squarely in the stomach. As I remember it, his kick was quite hard, perhaps hard enough to have knocked me backwards down the stairs (though it didn't). Was my brother aware of this possibility? Is this the clearest early memory I have of him because it was the one time (in my later childhood at least) that he fully expressed his murderous hostility towards me?

There is another incident from this same period that is almost certainly connected. I had brought two gerbils home from school in a cage for the weekend. Inspired by I knew not what dark impulse, I took them out of their cage, wrapped them inside a piece of clothing, and threw them violently across the room. Though they were unharmed physically, they were of course terrified; exercising such control over these defenseless creatures gave me a feeling of excitation, of sexual arousal, mixed up with confusion and guilt, and followed by shame and pity. I had no idea at that time why I had done such a thing. I assumed there was something wrong with me. Looking back now, however, it seems logical enough that all the helpless anger of those first few years under the tyranny of my brother had to come out somehow. I had treated those helpless gerbils exactly as I had been treated.

Being the receptacle of violence is like receiving a negative charge into the body. And, just as in the case of lightning, whoever the charge *stops at* receives the full jolt. If we receive such a charge, naturally we look for someone else to pass it onto, in order to relieve the pressure in our psyches. This is done by acting out the same scenes we were caught up in as children while taking the *reverse* position, that of the aggressor. And so we become the tormentor rather than the tormented: the slayer instead of the slain.

Clothes Without an Emperor

"I was frightened that I had become a self-parody—but without going to the trouble of acquiring a self first."
—The Brother, in his Memoirs, 2007

As we entered into adolescence, and like most boys, both my brother and I sought comfort through sex. Where my brother succeeded, I failed. What neither of us realized was how much we were following our father's example. The models of masculinity we are given in childhood define us, and there's no model more lasting than that of the father. Either we end up imitating his example or we rebel against it, but in either case, we are letting that example drive us. My brother eventually took to whoring, alcoholism, and entrepreneurship: just like our father. I wound up a reluctant celibate (virginal till I was 27) and a tea-totalling aesthete, living destitute on the streets as a vagabond: the negative image of my father and my brother. Hyper-sexuality and asexuality are complementary poles of the same distortion, the same wound; ditto extremes of high and low status. We were acting out a polarity consciousness, shouldering between us the load of our father's disowned unconscious.

My brother has been driven by pain his whole life. Anyone who reads his book cannot fail to hear the wail that sounds plaintive behind the endless string of one-liners. As he himself writes, he is a self-parody without a self. A shell of a man. Clothes without an emperor. Style devoid of substance. But the question he never raises, the question conspicuous for its absence, is: Why? What could have happened to drive him to seek refuge in purest artifice, in a semblance of superficiality at any cost? If this immersion in external darkness and depravity is what it takes for him to stay out of the depths of his own psyche, what must be lurking in those depths? What?

Few people who read his book will get the sense that my brother is trying to conceal anything or that he is attempting to paint a rose-tinted picture of himself. On the contrary, he is at pains to paint himself in the darkest tones imaginable. As a self-promoting, self-parodying author, he sets it up so that any charges aimed at him he has already leveled at himself. This is a cunning subterfuge: to expose oneself first in order to retain control over the exposure. On the other hand, when a person has something they wish to hide, an effective method is to reveal all sorts of information that most people would be ashamed to admit. This diverts our attention from whatever it is the author wishes to conceal. My brother reveals all the sordid details he can dredge up about himself (some of which are almost certainly exaggerated), as a way of ensuring that his real secret remains safe ~ perhaps even from himself.

Here is a man who has no qualms about telling tales of crack addiction, of eating his own feces and of being whipped with a belt while his head is submerged in a toilet bowl. So what about some of the things he chooses *not* to share with the world? What might *they* be? We can only imagine. There *is* one central aspect of his life that is conspicuously absent from his book, however: myself.

An autobiographer reveals most about himself by *what he chooses to omit.*

A Personal Attack, and an Impersonal Defense

"A paradox is the truth standing on its head in order to get attention."
—G.K. Chesterton

Here are two pieces that I wrote about my brother, at different phases in my life. The first is from 2007, after one of our many fallings out (a piece I never shared with anyone but our sister, written before I read his book):

The fact that my brother acts as his own pimp doesn't make him any less of a whore. My brother would no doubt have no objection to this, and would probably counter that prostitution is a perfectly noble profession. As a writer, my brother indeed possesses some of the sensibilities of a whore: he turns everything—his family and friends, his ex-wife, even his mother—into a "trick" for his own amusement, excuses to display his self-lacerating narcissism and his droll, nihilistic wit. In his glamorizing of prostitution, however, he conveniently ignores the core of self-loathing at the heart of so many ladies of the night. Is it not the same self-loathing at the center of his book: a self-loathing which can surely only be exasperated by the business of whoring?

My brother embodies the essence of fame—the glamorization of the superficial—and yet, as his many insights make plain, he is anything but superficial. His success represents the superior man's attempt to hide in a false persona that is nothing but "glamour"—illusion, self-serving vanity and the shallow gratification of ego. So it should come as no surprise if the world instantaneously approves and rewards such sly subterfuge. Yet his success raises the essential question: is recognition in itself more meaningful than what one becomes recognized for? Since the first thing he has done to gain the world's notice (at least since getting crucified) is to write his autobiography, he is in danger of following in the footsteps of Zsa-Zsa Gabor, and becoming famous for being famous. But underneath the painstakingly assembled veneer of glamorous corruption and glib cynicism lurks a soul in torment. I am only sorry that my brother chooses not to bare his soul as boldly and uncompromisingly as he bares his ass: he might present to the world more of a Greek tragedy, and less of a freak show.

On the other hand, here is one from 2009, when we were on friendly terms (a piece I sent to my brother as a gift, but never shared publically until now):

My brother (the man, not the work) is in the tradition of the old-style satirists, with one crucial difference. The old-style satirists, through their humorous prose, mocked society and its members, putting themselves outside and above it. For him, no such dividing line is permitted: the subject and the object of his satire are one and the same: himself. Largely eschewing the more traditional (and safer) methods of cultural artifice (novels, plays, paintings, and suchlike), which allow the artist a comfortable distance from the audience, he has turned himself into his own product. He invites his audience—implores it—to consume him, as a rare wine generously laced with strychnine, a voluptuous harlot riddled with sexually transmitted diseases. A living parody, he parades his glamorously deformed psyche before the world, and dares us to call him on it.

Self-publicity is not the end of his sorcery, however, merely the means. By being apparently willing to do anything (even get crucified) to earn the world's attention, my brother is taking a collective kind of dementia (the desire for fame at any cost) and stripping it bare. By showing us a man made almost wholly of clothing, he is letting the world see how dependent he is on artifact to conceal his true nature, and how utterly ineffective—and obvious—his disguises are. A cunningly assembled harlequin of self-doubt cloaked in self-aggrandizement, my brother almost perfectly (though perhaps unconsciously) mirrors the culture of self-worship in which he lives and breathes. He is a self-aware symptom of a sickening society that reflects back at us our own image. "This is what you could be if you dared," is only the first part of the message. The other part is: "This is what you are."

Jasun Horsley

Truth in a Top Hat: Insanity as Insistence

"I often wonder how it is that I who have always had a mind and the nerves and the history to go mad, have never actually done so."
—The Brother, in 1999

Here my brother asks a reasonable question, and I think there's a reasonable answer. There is more than one kind of insanity. There is the kind of madness my brother and I witnessed growing up with our mother, for example. The wailing harpy, hurling insults and hissing venom one minute, clawing at our father's legs and weeping the next. One defense against this sort of madness would be to take refuge in excessively rigid and inflexible modes of thought and action, the kind of obsessive-compulsive behavior exhibited by my brother, for example. Yet this would actually be the flip side of *the very same madness.*

Insisting on imposing our own version of reality onto existence, trying to become a law, a moral force, unto oneself, is also a kind of madness. My brother is an autocrat of ideology. He is a petty tyrant who enforces his version of reality with violence. For perhaps a third of my adult life, he hasn't been speaking to me. What was my crime? Daring to be myself in his presence. Being myself in his presence is something I have never found easy at the best of times. As adults, the same old order prevails: my brother has continued to impose his view of me onto my words and actions. Should I dare to stand up to him and tell him what I *really* think about any of this, the axe swiftly descends. There is really only one way to get along with my brother and that is to agree with him. If he doesn't like what you have to say, he either stonewalls it with anger or, more in keeping with his charismatic persona, he beats you to death with a relentless string of one-liners. It is very hard to maintain a serious conversation with someone who apparently wishes only to have an audience for their wit. My brother pretends this is simple vanity on his part; the truth is that there is a subtler and deeper rationale behind it. My brother is a master of disguising subtler and deeper agendas with a *seemingly transparent veneer.* That is his art, but also his sorcery.

My brother calls himself "an authentic phony." His point is that we are all fakes, but since he has the honesty and courage to admit it, that makes him less of a phony. Try suggesting, however, the possibility that an *authentic being* might exist beneath the façade of our constructed identities, and you risk incurring the tyrant's displeasure. He has put an awful lot of work and effort into perfecting his shallow façade: woe betide anyone who suggests that it might all be for nothing. His dandy-nihilism *insists* that surface is all there is, and that style is synonymous with substance. His identity is more lovingly constructed than ordinary mortals'; he is "a futile blaze of color in a futile, colorless world." Life is just meaningless chaos, so any belief in a design beneath the chaos is simply the vain projection of weaker, death-denying minds. It is not merely wrong, it is "unmanly." This is a convenient way to win arguments. The root of the word "royal" is *reality*. Kings and Queens got to decide what was real and what was not. "The best way to contradict me is to let me speak" quips my brother. This can be translated as—I am quite happy having a conversation with myself, thank you; your input is not required. Only I get to say what is real.

If my brother were more honest about it, what he would say is "If God existed, He would have introduced himself to me. Since He didn't, God obviously does not exist."

To become a God, Lucifer must first deny the existence of any God outside of himself.

It took me a while to recognize how these Luciferian qualities so obvious in my brother had actually become installed in my own psyche, and were playing out in subtler, more ambiguous ways. A while? Make that about forty years. In the interim, while this constant ideological war with my brother raged on, I became something of a megalomaniac myself. I believed I was The One. The creator of realities, Lucifer incarnate, the Messiah, the holder of the Key to the Mysteries. It's a curious fact that, while my brother dismissed my interest in UFOs, conspiracies, occultism, and divine forces as wish-fulfillment fantasy and delusional nonsense, he expressed approval and enjoyment at my more nakedly demented bid to become "the One." It was what we all wanted, he said. Actually, it was what *he* had wanted, as a child, and what I *got* to be the chosen one in our mother's eyes. So when I was acting out this mania, complete with designer black suit and shiny shoes (becoming a sort of postmodernist dandy simulacra), I was actually less an avatar for Lucifer than a vessel for *my brother's own unconscious.* Embodying his will without realizing it, I was becoming an unwitting reflection of his own narcissistic delirium.

If I Want Your Opinion, I'll Give it to You: Tyranny in Action

"As a dandy I have always elegantly acknowledged the fact that to live is to be defeated while steadfastly declining to surrender to that knowledge."
—The Brother, in his Memoirs, 2007

My brother has spent time in the AA and NA; his biggest stumbling block was acknowledging a force greater than himself. "I do not believe there is any force greater than myself" got a big laugh from the AA crowd. If the worth of a man is measured by what he values most highly, what can you say of the man who values nothing more highly than himself?

For one who believes in nothing, my brother's position is rigid and unbending, yet also untenable. Like all fanatics, it is doubt that strengthens his convictions. He not only disbelieves in everything (and disbelief is itself a form of belief), he despises those who do believe, and most of all those who *know*. If a man cannot recognize a deeper reality beneath the veneer of constructed identity, does that mean such a reality does not exist? If that man is my brother it does. Tell him you have experienced such a reality and that simply makes you a liar or a fool, or both.

Here's a not-quite random example of my brother's tyranny of disbelief: I once knew someone who claimed to have a dim memory of her birth. Since she was an intelligent and honest person (and although I remember little from before the age of six myself), I had no reason to doubt her. When I told my brother about it, he dismissed the idea scornfully. Since he could not remember that far back, no one could; it was simply a delusion, unworthy of further discussion. There are no rocks in the sky, so rocks cannot fall from the sky. Meteorites do not exist, and if you say they do, you are simply deluded. For an iconoclast, my brother is astonishingly conservative in his views. Anything outside of what he has cobbled together for his personal narrative must be dismissed as nonsense, be it God, UFOs, or Children.

This may be the key to my brother, and to his life-long art of creating distorted surrogate realities and false narratives. Oddly enough, it often seems to revolve around children and memories of childhood. To give another example, my brother (with me at least) has also insisted that children do not really exist, in the strict sense of the word, because they have no minds of their own, no personalities. Paradoxically, he also claims that, as a child, he was the exact same person he is now. This is more of the same insistence: since only the constructed identity is real, children, not having yet constructed their identities, cannot exist. If they did exist, that would mean that some sort of consciousness were possible outside the confines of the sovereign ego-self. To acknowledge that possibility would be tantamount to allowing for the existence of the divine: a substance beyond the surface, content independent of style. Through these tiny chinks in the armor, the light of truth sneaks in.

My brother argues, therefore, that anything that happens to us as children can have no lasting impact upon us, because we weren't "real people" then. He has also argued (to me), just as passionately, that no harm could come to a small child from being sexually molested. This, he insists, is merely the imposition of moral assumptions onto an otherwise neutral and "harmless" experience. Why would he argue such an absurd point so virulently, you might ask? You might answer that this is also all part of the same insistence. Since children are not innocent or pure to begin with (in fact they are nothing at all), they cannot be violated. Where nothing is sacred, nothing can be profaned. I would suggest, however, that we are now getting to the very root of this insistence, and so must be careful not to mistake an effect for a cause. A more piercing question might be: did something of the kind happen to him? Or did he perhaps commit a similar kind of act? Is this why he is so heavily invested in a system of belief that denies the sanctity of children? Because his own sanctity was violated? Where there is a smoke screen of such thickness and stench, it is reasonable to look for a fire behind it.

The idea of childhood trauma is beneath my brother. It is the product of an overly analytical age, of minds that have become enamored of psychotherapy and are anxious to pass the buck and play the role of victim (a word he despises). *He* had a difficult childhood and *he* got over it. Why can't everyone else? Blaming our parents for our adult distortions is "dreary" and lacks style. This isn't simply about him refusing to blame his parents (a respectable enough position): he will not allow that such early experiences have *any significant impact at all*. Not on him at least. He is, after all, a dandy. A *self-created* man.

Anyone who has observed this underworld dandy in action or read his book and interviews, anyone who has even the most rudimentary knowledge of psychology, can attest that my brother is very far from being "over his childhood." Consider it thus: If a man's body is covered with scars and yet he has no memory of how the scars got there; and if the man knows for a fact that he spent some years in the war when he was younger; isn't it a reasonably safe deduction that at least some of those scars are the result of wounds inflicted during that war? It might even be deduced from the *lack* of memory (as well as the severity of the scars) just how traumatic those events must have been. So it is with the psyche. If there are scars found therein, with no clear memory of how they got there, there is only one logical place to look.

My brother's willful ignorance and denial of the impact of those early years on his psyche doesn't reduce that impact. If anything, it only makes it all the more profound. Kept in the unconscious, the unprocessed trauma gets to work away in secret, and do the most possible damage. What is left on the surface? Little more than a well-dressed marionette, singing and dancing to the shrill and grisly backbeat of long-suppressed, long-denied childhood wounds. It is a freak show in which the freak on show was created, from birth, to be exactly what it is.

Family Circle, Family Secrets

"As a child my insides were full of nightmares, of impossible battles, terrifying anxieties of blood, pain, aloneness, darkness and destruction, mixed with limitless desires, sensations of unspeakable beauty, majesty, awe and mystery. Sometimes my adolescence was spent in quiet but dark revolt. And yet, these were the happiest days of my life. What made them great was Mother."
—The Brother, in his Memoirs, 2007

Besides the paragraph quoted earlier (in which he describes his violent treatment of me), there is only one other description of myself in my brother's book. It is equally telling, though for somewhat different reasons.

"[Our paternal grandparents' house] had even dodgier visitors. A pedophile friend of Grandfather's, his face riddled with cancer, once took a shine to Brother. Brother, as a child, had one of those faces of marvelous beauty which stopped strangers in the streets, so a pedophile invited into the family circle could hardly have been expected to be indifferent. I detested his ingratiating manner, his obsequious compliments—but solely because they weren't directed at me."

Two things can be inferred from this. The first is that my brother's sovereignty was threatened above all *by my physical beauty*. Nothing could outshine him and rob him of the attention he deserved more than this. It's easy to imagine how he must have brooded each time a stranger stopped us in the street to admire me—a cruel reminder of his having been supplanted. (Before I came along, strangers had perhaps stopped to admire *him* in the street.) So it can hardly be a coincidence that, as an adult, my brother relies upon *his physical beauty as his chief virtue.* As a dandy, his appearance is his currency. With his outlandish and elaborate dress, he is guaranteed to get all the attention he craved as a child and to never be upstaged again. His appearance is so extravagant, in fact, that strangers have been known to applaud him when he walks into a room.

The second thing that comes clearly into focus in the above passage is somewhat darker and more disturbing: the notion that, because of my child's beauty, I was *a natural bait for sexual deviants.*

"A pedophile invited into the family circle . . ."

Was this an isolated incident, or is it the tip of a family iceberg? In the liberal-socialist background which we grew up in (the "family circle" that of my father's father), there was no shortage of sexual libertines hanging around. Judging by the above, a predilection for young boys was not considered a reason to be barred access to the circle either. In my parents' house, drunken parties were frequent, and although they were less than Roman orgies, there was no shortage of alcoholic excess and, knowing our father, probably a degree of sexual excess also.

None of this proves anything. But it does indicate that there was ample opportunity for sexual meddling to have occurred, either with myself or my brother (or both). Add to this the various strange behaviors exhibited by both my brother and myself in adulthood—behavior quite in keeping with symptoms of sexual abuse—and the possibility, while still only a possibility, becomes more tangible. The truth may never be known. But to assume that nothing of the kind occurred because there is no record of it is perhaps no more intelligent than to dismiss the idea because no one in our family has ever spoken about it. People generally *don't* speak about such things, for obvious reasons. And incidents of this nature are very often entirely forgotten later in life, for equally obvious reasons, particularly if the abuse occurs very young. *Forgetting is the most effective means of coping that we have.*

The only clues that remain, then, are those found in our patterns of behavior as adults. Though he may hate me for life for saying it, my brother is a text book case of how victims of child abuse wind up behaving as adults. He is unusual only in being so extreme; in fact, he is practically a caricature. So then, is this what all his ostentatious manifestations of amorality and darkness, compulsive, self-harming behavior, sexual depravity and licentiousness, are *really* about? Is this what, unconsciously, he is drawing the world's attention to: whatever he was forced to keep secret as a child, so secret that it wound up becoming a secret even to himself?

On the Run from Intimacy: The Dandy as the Quintessential Mother's Boy

"Having a secret life is exhilarating. I also have problems with unpaid-for sex. I am repulsed by the animality of the body, by its dirt and decay. The horror for me is the fact that the sublime, the beautiful and the divine are inextricable from basic animal functions. For some reason money mitigates this. Because it is anonymous."
—The Brother, in 2004

Running through his memoirs, like blood from an open wound onto every page, is my brother's deep fear of intimacy, and of the vulnerability which it brings. This is particularly evident in his views on women. Naturally, growing up with a crazed and drunken mother would have made it highly unsafe for him to experience a loving connection to women. (This is something I can also testify to also.) There is nothing comparative to the vulnerability of a child, and the wounding that occurs while we are in this vulnerable state creates enough scar tissue to keep us closed for life. My brother's book testifies to this wounding. It shows how he has been at pains to avoid intimacy and vulnerability at any cost, but *most especially around women*. Of *course* he would be at pains to avoid it: they might turn on him at any moment, just as our mother did. It is perfectly natural for him to be drawn to prostitutes as the safest surrogate for a genuine experience of intimacy. A prostitute must harden and close herself up emotionally, simply in order to survive. No wonder my brother identifies with them: he has done the same thing, and for the exact same reasons. As his own "product," he is even in much the same line of work. Yet my brother's elaborate and eloquent philosophy of self-justification and denial betrays itself at every turn, often deliberately. "The best way to contradict me is to let me speak." The absurdity of his arguments is often unintentional, however, as when he calls "Prostitutes the most open and honest creatures on God's earth." Does he really believe this? Does he also believe it when they fake their orgasms for him? Is that part of the bargain? Mutual enjoyment would entail a real connection, and this would mean genuine intimacy, of soul as well as body. This is most certainly *not* part of the deal.

Jesus Christ also had a predilection for prostitutes, and I suspect my brother's interest in fallen women goes a fair bit deeper than he lets on. The desire to save a fallen woman (who stands in for the *anima*, his very own soul) fuels the fantasies of many romantic males who suffer from arrested emotional development. It is the desire to play Christ to Mary Magdalene, to rescue the whore from her sins (and from the judging eyes of the mob), and to redeem her with his healing touch and sacred cock. Such a romantic desire would have been first sown in my brother's heart by the countless times he saw our mother falling down (literally and figuratively), and lacked the

73

strength or wherewithal to lift her up and carry her to safety.

Women and prostitutes are virtual synonyms in my brother's world. Here he is expounding on both:

"Part of me used to enjoy the deception. There was something about the poverty of desire with one's girlfriend. *Sex without betrayal I found meaningless.*"

This is a pattern sourced in our childhood: our father cheated on our mother, and our mother responded by taking another man into her bed. The things we grow up witnessing are our yardsticks for reality because we have nothing to juxtapose them with. They are what constitutes normality. As a result, we seek out similar patterns of behavior as adults, because they are safer, but also more emotionally charged—more "meaningful"—to us. In his memoir, my brother describes two relationship triangles that are key to his narrative, triangles between himself, a woman, and another man. Such a triangle is in fact precisely what we grew up with, when our mother had two "husbands" simultaneously. Perhaps more pertinent to this work, we were also part of such a triangle: the one created by the rivalry between the two of us *for our mother's affections.*

My brother writes of sexual love: "Without cruelty there was no banquet."

Our first experience of sexual love was that which we witnessed between our parents, and it was indeed both opulent and cruel.

"What I hate with women generally is the intimacy, *the invasion of my innermost space,* the slow strangulation of my art. . . . When I love somebody, I feel sort of trapped."

Here he describes precisely how we both would have felt around our mother as children, as she fluctuated between cold indifference, irrational rage, smothering affection, and drunken sentimentality.

"The whore fuck is the purest fuck of all. . . . I love the artificial paradise; the anonymity; using money, the most impersonal instrument of intimacy, to buy the most personal act of intimacy. Lust over love, sensation over security, and *to fall into a woman's arms without falling into her hands.*" (Italics mine.)

That first, imprinting experience of our mother was one in which intimacy was potentially terrifying, in which security threatened us with suffocation, and in which we would have been powerless to defend against her unpredictable outbursts. No wonder my brother only feels safe with prostitutes. (And no wonder I was mostly celibate for the first 35 years of my life.)

My brother practices a contrived form of honesty. It is a kind of selective truth-telling that is invariably self-serving. He spins the truth in such a way that it is as effective to his ends as lying would be, yet with the added advantage of closely resembling honesty. By parading his flaws before the world, for example, he renders himself exempt from having to look at these flaws himself. He exaggerates his countless neuroses and turns them into vices; and by glamorizing his vices, he makes them seem almost like virtues. He *owns* his vices and uses them to define himself, rather than owning *up* to them and moving beyond them (which is what maturity consists of). It is the behavior of a child who longs only for attention and doesn't care how he gets it. But my brother is a child in the body of a 47-year-old man. By his own admission, he is "a buffoon in a velvet cocoon." He is a small child's idea of what being a man might be like; fittingly, he has created a persona that (for all its sordid darkness) is geared above all to pleasing his mother: a man of wit and charm, of great beauty and social graces, a poet and a romantic. A dandy. While as a father or husband, he is every woman's worst nightmare, he remains, in our mother's own words, "the perfect date."

Like all dandies, he is the quintessential mother-bonded male. The one that will never get away. No matter how many lovers he takes or whores he sleeps with, he will always return to his first love. His mother, his keeper.

"Crack is the whore. Heroin is the mother. Together they make a mother with a cunt. It doesn't get any better than that."
—The Brother, in his Memoirs, 2007.

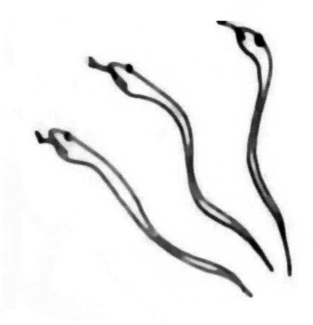

Cracking the Cosmic Egg

"It seems you have been living two lives. One of these lives has a future. The other does not."
—Agent Smith, to Thomas Anderson, *The Matrix*

The myth of Cain and Abel is echoed by that of Esau and Jacob and (more esoterically) of Lucifer and Christ. Cain/Esau/Lucifer is the first-born, but also the disfavored son. (In Lucifer's case he is the "brightest angel" who is also the rejected Son of God.) Why is the first-born or brightest angel also the one that is spurned? What are these myths trying to tell us? Lucifer's fall sowed the seed of original sin; Christ came as the redeemer to die for our sins. An occult reading of the Cain/Abel story is represented in the Tarot by The Lovers card: Cain is the masculine side of the alchemical marriage, Abel the feminine. The blood shed and the blow struck is that of sexual union, the wound that of the bloody vagina. In such a reading, although it is Abel who is wounded by Cain's "club," this is the necessary means for Cain's essence to enter into Abel. So then it is Cain who "dies," in order to sow the seed of the next generation. (This is why "dandies do not breed," because to do so would be to become obsolete.) Like Agent Smith and Neo in *The Matrix*, Tyler Durden and the narrator in *Fight Club*, or Maximus and Commodus in *Gladiator*, the two antagonists are absorbed into one, that a third being may come into existence, a composite of the two. Cain is the outermost part of consciousness—the ego self—and Abel is the innermost, the soul or essence. Cain is the male, Abel is the female; the synthesis of the two is *the child.*

To enter into the Kingdom of God, we must become as little children. It is harder for a rich man to enter Heaven than for a camel to pass through the eye of a needle.

The constructed identity is a protective shell for the consciousness of the child to hide inside, as it extends into the hostile environment that is its world. It is a shell inside which the bird of our innermost being can grow to full strength, and begin to move. This movement is meant to crack the shell when the time is right (probably in adolescence), so the child can become a man. The constructed identity is there to hold a space for the child-self of pure consciousness to move into and through, into its full expression in manhood. This never happens in our world, however. What happens in our world is that the constructed identity, instead of giving this space over to the innermost, *takes it for itself.*

Lucifer usurps the throne and chooses to reign in Hell rather than serve in Heaven. There is then no way for our innermost being to move or to express itself, since it remains trapped inside the constructed identity, like a bird stuck inside an egg. To crack that egg of identity *from the outside* then becomes the only way for our being to live. We must slay ourselves using whatever means available. The harder and more rigid the constructed identity becomes, the more brittle and fragile, and the more fiercely it defends itself with its beliefs, its insistence on a *false narrative*. In the end, all it takes is the gentlest touch of truth in the right place for that egg to crack open. This is birth for the true being; but, as often as not, it is death to the person.

Writing this story has been an act of self-slaying for its author. These fragments are the pieces of the shell that I leave behind.

The End of Sovereignty

"The time for honoring yourself will soon be at an end."
—Maximus to Commodus, *Gladiator*

I am not interested in slaying my brother, but I am compelled to slay myself. Because my own constructed identity was designed primarily as a defense against my brother's hostile, murderous presence in those early years, this led to my becoming an unconscious imitation of him. Reflecting this, he also became *the living embodiment of my own distortions*. By confronting that distortion head-on and gazing unflinchingly at the image it reflects back at me, I am able to see myself as I am, and to see, clearly and finally, that I am *not* that. I never was that. This narrative is a false narrative. The matrix cannot tell me who I am.

In this moment, the mirror of self-reflection shatters into a thousand pieces. The bubble bursts, the egg cracks open.

This book has been my way of addressing that internal critic voice of my brother, once and for all, giving it what it wants, and allowing it to be still. If I can get *this* one past that psychic guardian, it will no longer have anything left to guard. The dialogue will be at an end.

The moment we let in whatever it is that our identity armor was constructed to keep out, the armor begins to crumble. Like the skin of a snake, it no longer serves any purpose to our beings. What we needed protection from as children, we do not need protection from as adults. In fact, what we most fear as adults is total exposure, total vulnerability, which is the very state we were born into that proved so devastating to us, all those years ago. Now, what we most fear is what we most desire: the touch of our innermost being. All our defenses cannot keep that touch away, because the truth is inside us. As it begins to move, the shell—which is all we ever thought we were—begins to tremble and crack.

There is nothing we can do except to give in gracefully.

There are only two possible responses to an encounter with reality. Either we surrender, or we stand our ground and suffer the ignominy of defeat. To know that to live is to be defeated and to decline to surrender to that knowing is the original sin, Lucifer's defiance: "Not Thy will, but *my* will be done!" It is an empty show of bravado, yet one that creates a Hell in the heart of Paradise, an isolate, self-contained reality with no room for truth to enter into it, a world that offers the cold and lonely solace of being, at least, our own version of reality. It is our own self-created narrative, in which we can at long last be Kings.

Ask Macbeth where such a path leads. He will tell you what a life of service to the sovereign self consists of. His words echo the mood of my brother's tale, "a tale told by an idiot, full of sound and fury, signifying nothing."

My Brother, My Ally: Traditions of Castration

"Nothing on the face of this earth—and I do mean nothing—is half so dangerous as a children's story that happens to be real, and you and I are wandering blindfolded through a myth devised by a maniac."
— Master Li Kao (T'ang Dynasty)

In myths about brothers, there is invariably animosity between the two. In these stories, the malevolent brother generally depends upon the trusting naiveté of the other brother in order to work his wiles more effectively. This malevolence or trickiness invariably backfires, however, so that innocence and guilelessness eventually prevails (as in the story of the Tortoise and the Hare). Besides the Bible stories already cited, there is an older, more abstract myth-story that, for its very lack of realism, gets closer to the psychic reality of my own narrative. It is the story of Set and Osiris.

Told simply: Set, jealous of his brother Osiris being chosen to rule over Egypt, plots to kill him. Set throws a party for his brother and prepares a trap for him, building a beautiful sarcophagus (coffin) and offering to make a gift of it to whoever fits inside it. He has already built the coffin to match his brother's dimensions, however, and of course his earnest brother Osiris, guileless and wholly unsuspecting, climbs inside the coffin. Set slams it shut and, with his cohorts, whisks the King away and throws the sarcophagus (weighted down with lead) into the Nile. Osiris' Wife Isis saves the body and buries it, but Set finds it, and this time he cuts the body into 14 parts and scatters them throughout Egypt.

The second part of the myth entails Isis' dedicated search for her dead husband's body parts in order to put him back together again. She manages to find all the parts except one, his penis, which Set has thrown into the Nile and which was subsequently eaten by a fish. (In some accounts, Set himself eats it.) Undeterred, Isis forges a surrogate phallus out of gold, and thereby completes Osiris' restoration and resurrection.

The third part of the story entails Isis' impregnation (via the golden phallus) with a son, Horus, and Osiris' departure to Amenta, where he becomes the Lord of the Dead. Horus grows up to be a great warrior and seeks vengeance for his father's murder. He confronts his uncle Set and slays him, thereby restoring balance to the land. In some stories, Horus is actually Set's younger brother, making Horus in effect the resurrected Osiris: Osiris' death is his "translation" to a higher realm of being, via the act of giving a son to Isis.

As everyone who has ever enjoyed an action-adventure yarn knows, there can be no real story without an antagonist to get things moving. Without Judas and Pontius Pilate to get Jesus up on the cross, there would have been no resurrection; without Agent Smith, Neo would never have become the One. What's implicit in these stories is the idea that the villain of the piece—the apparent enemy of the protagonist—is really acting as *an agent of transformation*, both his own (via death) and that of the hero, through rebirth. The story of Osiris and Set illustrates this much more clearly than that of Abel and Cain. Bringing it back to my own story, symbolically speaking, and even to a degree literally (though I may never know to what degree), my brother, like Set, put his hands on my masculinity and rendered me impotent. What he did to me was a sort of psychic castration, an energetic dismemberment. Since I was a threat to his masculinity, he became a threat to mine. And as in the story of Osiris and Set, it was not a contest of equals. My brother used his trickery to take advantage of my innocence. I lay passively down inside the trap he laid for me. He took a hold of my cradle (pram), pushed it down the hill, and declared me dead.

Fearful Symmetry

"Opposition is true friendship."
—William Blake, Proverbs of Hell

There is another of my early memories that seems significant at this juncture, one that happened around the same time as the stomach blow. I had made myself a fake cigarette, using a rolled up piece of paper or cardboard, and I was pretending to smoke it at the kitchen table. My brother saw it and began to mock me for my childishness and naiveté. I can still remember the vitriol behind his words and how it scalded me. What he expressed so viscerally with his verbal attack was complete disgust at my attempting to be a man or act like an adult. I didn't know anything about it, his words inferred, because only *he* knew what it was to be a man (or to smoke a cigarette; he probably had smoked himself by that time). Since our father smoked tobacco while he was still living with us, I was probably trying to copy his behavior. That would have added an even more personal charge to my brother's scorn. I could never be like (or replace) our father; only *he* could do that. He was right: I never did become like our father.

In this case it's safe to say that a cigarette is not just a cigarette. Once again I had been "castrated."

My brother is the biggest asshole I have ever known. He's always been that way and he probably always will be. But if writing this piece has allowed me to see anything, it is that he never really had any choice about it. My angelic existence forced him into the only role left for him, that of diabolic opposition. He became an asshole out of self-preservation; and in the end, self-preservation makes assholes of us all. To make amends with my brother is something I have tried my whole life. How do you make amends with someone who acts like an asshole? As Osiris discovered, earnestness is no match for trickery.

This book is me owning my inner asshole.

I threatened by brother's masculinity simply by being. In return, he threatened my masculinity by *doing*. Since it is my mere *being* that threatens my brother, the only way to approach him as a *doing* and *not* be a threat, is to match his own doing and be an asshole. Because it is my way of being that has threatened him and forced him to act (and to see himself) as an asshole his whole life, now let the shoe be on the other foot.

And let the lamb devour the lion.

Whatever we inherit in this life is what we have been given. It's our "lot." Whatever my brother may say about it, we are more than just persons scrambling for sovereignty in a hostile environment. We are also fragments of the divine, evolving through adversity and restriction. For the deepest possible experience of ourselves, as consciousness within this material realm, inside this mortal coil, we naturally seek out those circumstances that allow us to come to the fullness of our potential. If myths, as psychological blueprints, show us anything it is that nothing is random. We come into this world like unfinished, partly written stories. All the elements are there, but it is up to us, that tiny fragment of self-awareness that allows for "free will," to figure out how the pieces fit together and come up with an ending.

The primary obstacle to this is the illusion that, once we are fully grown, we are finished products, and that there is nothing we can do within the limitations of our "fixed" identity, besides seeking external happiness, worldly status, or personal sovereignty. The secondary mistake is when we look at our limitations as something outside of ourselves to be lamented, and see our wounds exclusively as the result of what was "done to us" as children (or later in life). These wounds then become what is holding us back and keeping us from being what we could be, if only things had been different. But the reverse is really the case: these wounds are cracks in the egg of our constructed identities. It is only by going all the way into them that we can pass through them to the other side, into a new way of being.

Being dismantled psychically is the only chance we have of getting put back together *in the right way*. It's how the unfinished story of our mythic unfolding gets finished. The agent of our wounding and dismemberment—be he Set, or Cain, or Judas, or Agent Smith or Commodus—is the most essential ingredient in the soul's alchemy. My brother has been my greatest ally in this life. By wounding my sexuality, he allowed me to see the distortion that already existed in me, because it was there even before the original wound was inflicted. It is a distortion that exists *in all of us,* because it is generational. So who is the victim here? By being born, I caused a deep wound to my brother's sexuality. He struck out, in rage and pain, to wound me back. As a child, he didn't know any different. We were both innocent. But that innocence is far behind us now.

So now I reach out, with the gentlest of touches, to push softly on the wall of the shell between us, to watch it crack and crumble. And with it goes the lifelong illusion of adversity and animosity and of *difference,* to reveal ~ what?

The petty tyrant was just a paper tiger after all.

And it reaches its most gorgeous apotheosis now, by this act of catching fire.

"Tyger! Tyger! burning bright
In the forests of the night,
What immortal hand or eye
Could frame thy fearful symmetry?"
—William Blake

Through the Looking Glass, Darkly

"And Cain said unto the LORD, My punishment is greater than I can bear. Behold, thou hast driven me out this day from the face of the earth; and from thy face shall I be hid; and I shall be a fugitive and a vagabond in the earth; and it shall come to pass, that every one that findeth me shall slay me."
—Genesis 4: 10-14

Dear Brother

There is no sense in asking you to forgive me. That would be dishonest. I did what I had to do, and what I did was true, not just to me but also to you.

If one child receives a parent's blessing, then is the other child cursed. If God's love is conditional, then to Hell with God's love, and to Hell with hers.

Sticks and stones may break your bones. But it takes words to strike the killing blow.

Somewhere along the way we switched roles. I crossed a line and found myself on the other side of the mirror. If you, my brother, were my enemy, then my enemy was myself. By submitting to your violence I became the violator.

But I was not cut out for murder; that was your calling. All I ever did here was to restore the balance.

This is not an act of vengeance, but of mercy.

Would you hate the mirror for refusing to give in gracefully to illusion?

Can you not see this? Are you not Abel?

Then you see why that makes me Cain.

Jasun Horsley

Jasun Horsley is the author of several books under various names. He is a multimedia storyteller and trans-therapist who divides his time between dream and reality. He is currently exploring "extra-consensual perception," enlightenment, and the mystery of autism.

His website is http://www.auticulture.com

Made in the USA
Columbia, SC
06 May 2019